It's a Handwriting heatwave from CGP!

Learning how to write neatly is a really important skill in Year 1, and the only way to tackle it is practice, practice and more practice...

That's where this CGP book comes in. It's packed with bright and colourful handwriting exercises for every day of summer term.

And of course, we've included helpful guidelines and plenty of examples — perfect for sharpening up pupils' handwriting skills, one day at a time!

What CGP is all about

Our sole aim here at CGP is to produce the highest quality books — carefully written, immaculately presented and dangerously close to being funny.

Then we work our socks off to get them out to you — at the cheapest possible prices.

Contents

☑ Use the tick boxes to help keep a record of which pages have been attempted.

Published by CGP

ISBN: 978 1 78908 544 0

Editors: Eleanor Crabtree, Mary Falkner, Rob Hayman, Camilla Sheridan and Hayley Thompson.
Reviewers: Stephanie Lake and Adele Lemin.

With thanks to Sharon Keeley-Holden and Gareth Mitchell for the proofreading.
With thanks to Jan Greenway for the copyright research.

Cover image and graphics used throughout the book © www.edu-clips.com.

Printed by Elanders Ltd, Newcastle upon Tyne.
Based on the classic CGP style created by Richard Parsons.

How to Use this Book

- This book contains 60 pages of daily handwriting practice.

- It's split into 12 sections — that's roughly one section for each week of the Year 1 Summer term.

- A week is made up of 5 pages, so there's one for every school day of the term (Monday – Friday).

- Each page should take about 10 minutes to complete.

- The term starts off by recapping the alphabet, capital letters and numbers. The rest of the term involves tracing and copying whole words, including common exception words from the National Curriculum.

- On Day 5 of each week, there is a more varied task. This may involve tracing and copying whole sentences or groups of words with a particular theme.

- A typical page looks like this:

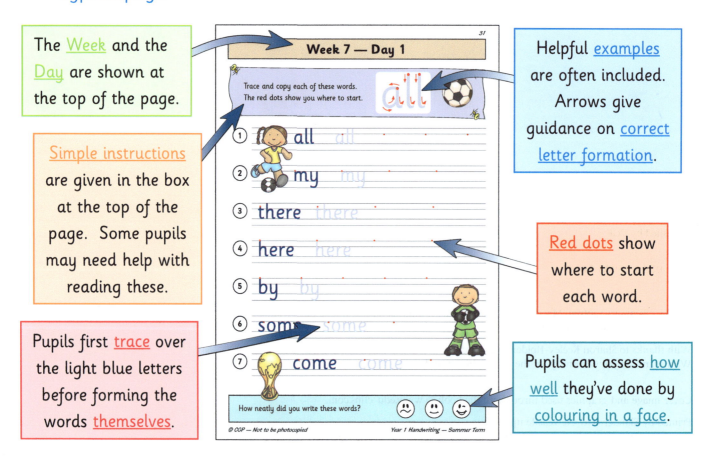

The Week and the Day are shown at the top of the page.

Simple instructions are given in the box at the top of the page. Some pupils may need help with reading these.

Pupils first trace over the light blue letters before forming the words themselves.

Helpful examples are often included. Arrows give guidance on correct letter formation.

Red dots show where to start each word.

Pupils can assess how well they've done by colouring in a face.

If you are a parent or guardian using this book at home with your child, you should bear in mind that different schools have different handwriting styles (e.g. 'k' instead of 'k'). You should check with the school to see how each letter is written. In this book, some of the letters have flicks at the bottom in preparation for joined-up writing.

Week 1 — Day 1

Trace each letter and then copy it.
Start at the red dot each time.

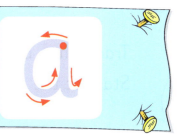

① 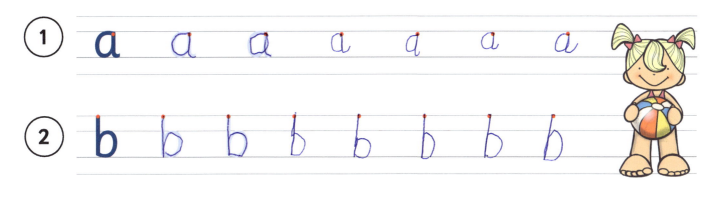 a a a a a a a

② b b b b b b b b

③ c c c c c c c c

④  d d d d d d d d

⑤ e e e e e e e e

⑥  f f f f f f f f

⑦ g g g g g g g g

How did you get on with these letters?

Year 1 Handwriting — Summer Term

Week 1 — Day 2

Trace, then copy, each of these letters.
Start at the red dot each time.

1. h h h h h h h
2. i i i i i i i
3. j j j j j j j
4. k k k k k k k
5. l l l l l l l
6. m m m m m m m
7. n n n n n n n

How easy did you find this page?

Week 1 — Day 3

Practise tracing and copying all of these letters.
Remember to start at the red dots.

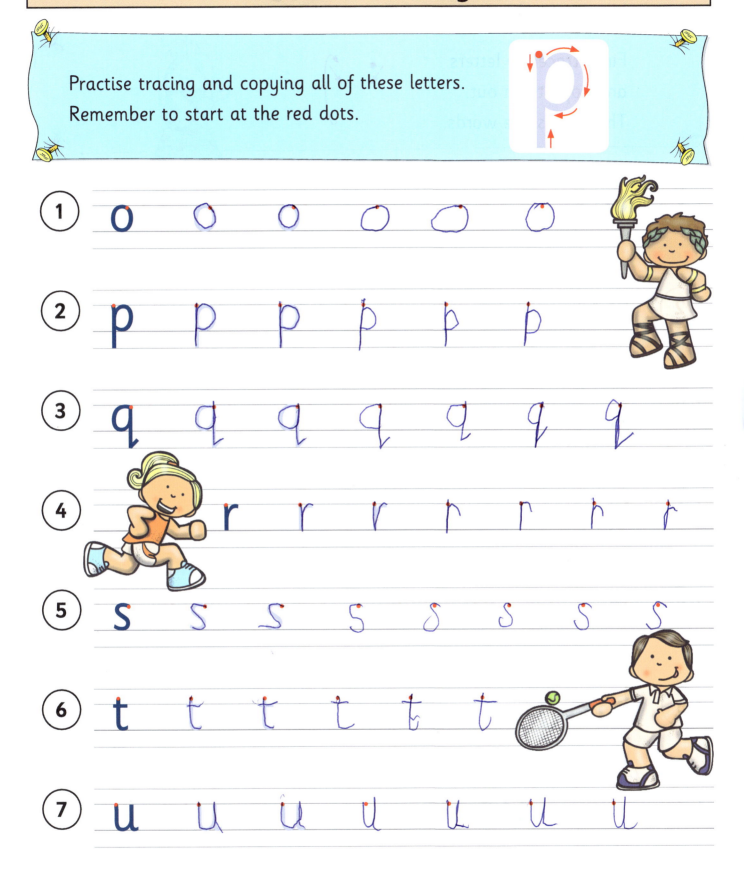

1. o o o o o o

2. p p p p p p

3. q q q q q q q

4. r r r r r r r

5. s s s s s s s

6. t t t t t t

7. u u u u u u u

How did you find these letters?

Year 1 Handwriting — Summer Term

Week 1 — Day 4

First, trace the letters and copy them out.
Then, try some words.

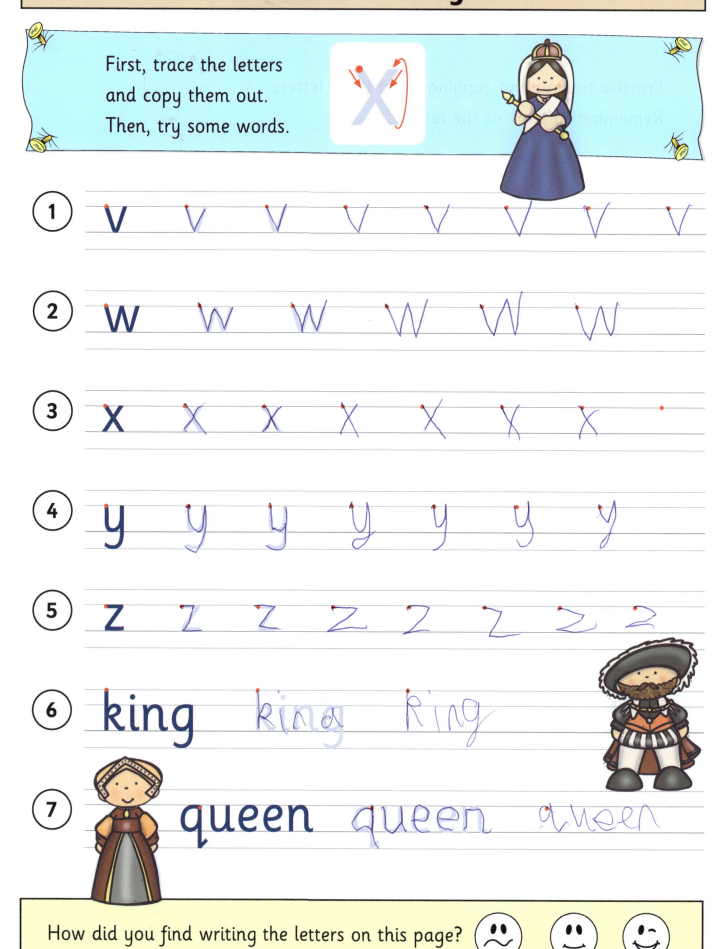

1. v v v v v v v v

2. w w w w w w

3. x x x x x x x

4. y y y y y y y

5. z z z z z z z z

6. king king king

7. queen queen queen

How did you find writing the letters on this page?

Week 1 — Day 5

Trace this packing list for a holiday, then copy it out.
Start each word at a red dot.

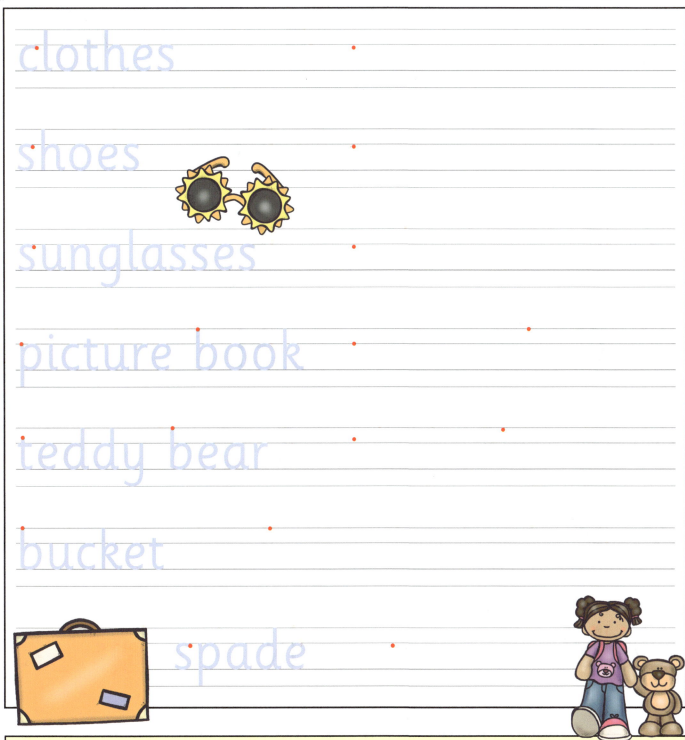

clothes

shoes

sunglasses

picture book

teddy bear

bucket

spade

Colour in a face to show how you got on!

Year 1 Handwriting — Summer Term

Week 2 — Day 1

Trace each capital letter and then write it yourself. You will need to lift your pencil off the page for most of these letters.

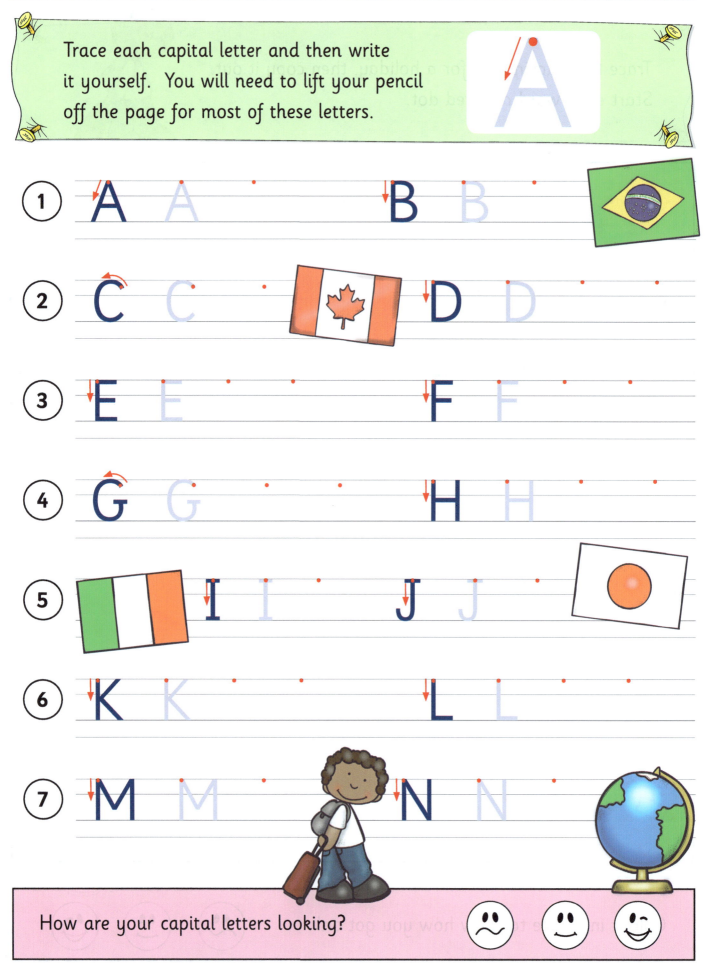

1. A A B B

2. C C D D

3. E E F F

4. G G H H

5. I I J J

6. K K L L

7. M M N N

How are your capital letters looking?

Week 2 — Day 2

Trace and then copy each of the letters. You will need to lift your pencil off the page for some of them.

① O O   P P

② Q Q   R R

③ S S   T T

④ U U   V V

⑤ W W

⑥ X X   Y Y

⑦ Z Z

How well did you do with these capital letters?

Week 2 — Day 3

Trace and then copy each of these numbers. You will need to lift your pencil off the page for 4 and 5.

1. 0 0

2. 1 1

3. 2 2

4. 3 3

5. 4 4

6. 5 5

7. 6 6

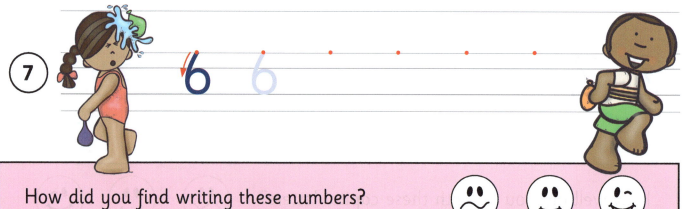

How did you find writing these numbers?

Week 2 — Day 4

Trace and then copy out these numbers and sums. You will need to lift your pencil off the page for the '+' and '=' signs.

1. 7 7

2. 8 8

3. 9 9

4.  10 10

5. 1 + 2 = 3

6. 7 + 1 = 8

7. 4 + 5 = 9

How do you feel about writing numbers?

Year 1 Handwriting — Summer Term

Week 2 — Day 5

Trace and then copy out this invite to a birthday party.

To Donna,

Please come to my party

at Beverley ice rink.

It is on Monday at 11:30.

How does your invite look?

Week 3 — Day 1

Trace over each of these words.
Then, copy them.
Start each word at the red dot.

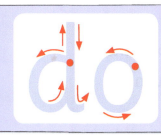

(1) do *do*   ·   ·   ·

(2) the *the*   ·   ·   ·

(3) to *to*   ·   ·   ·

(4) of *of*   ·   ·   ·

(5) said *said*   ·   ·

(6) says *says*   ·   ·

(7) are *are*   ·   ·

How did you find this page?

Year 1 Handwriting — Summer Term

Week 3 — Day 2

Trace and then copy these words with 'oo' in them.

moon

1. moon   moon

2. spoon   spoon

3. hoot   hoot

4. spooky   spooky

5. loop   loop

6. tooth   tooth

7. zoo   zoo

How did you get on with these words?

Week 3 — Day 3

Here are some different 'oo' words.
Trace and then copy them.

① book   book

②  look   look

③ cook   cook

④ good   good

⑤ wool   wool

⑥ foot   foot

⑦ cookie   cookie

Did you trace and copy these words neatly?

Year 1 Handwriting — Summer Term

Week 3 — Day 4

Practise tracing and then copying these 'ou' words. Make sure you start at the red dot each time.

1. loud loud

2. hour hour

3. sound sound

4. cloud cloud

5. house house

6. found found

7. shout shout

How did it go? Time to choose a face.

Week 3 — Day 5

Trace and then copy these facts about the Moon.

The Moon is made of rock.

It goes around the Earth.

You can see it after dark,

when it is not cloudy.

How did you get on with the facts on this page?

Year 1 Handwriting — Summer Term

Week 4 — Day 1

Trace each of these words and then copy them out.
Start at the red dot each time.

1. is   is

2. I   I

3. his   his

4. her   her

5. has   has

6. was   was

7. were   were

How did you do with these words?

Week 4 — Day 2

First, trace each word.
Then, copy it out.
Start at the red dot each time.

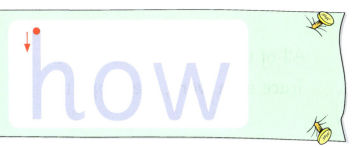

1. how   how

2. cow   cow

3. now   now

4. howl   howl

5.  owl   owl

6. brown   brown

7. down   down

How did you get on with today's words?

Year 1 Handwriting — Summer Term

Week 4 — Day 3

All of these words have 'or' in.
Trace each word, then copy it.

born

(1) born born

(2) for for

(3) cord cord

(4) fork fork

(5) corn corn

(6) short short

(7) horse horse

Could you trace and copy all of the words neatly?

Week 4 — Day 4

Trace each of these 'ore' words and then copy them out.

 more

1. more   more

2. wore   wore

3. score   score

4. shore   shore

5. store   store

6. core   core

7. before   before

How did you get on with these words?

Year 1 Handwriting — Summer Term

Week 4 — Day 5

This poem is about a snail. Trace each line of the poem and then copy it out below.

I have my own pet snail.

He really likes to climb.

He leaves a shiny trail

And covers me in slime.

Did you trace and copy the poem neatly?

Week 5 — Day 1

Trace and then copy these words as practice.

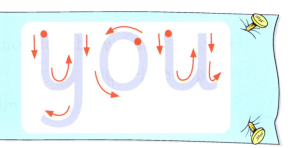

1. you   you

2. your   your

3.    we   we

4. be   be

5. he   he

6. she   she

7.    me   me

How did you get on with these words?

Year 1 Handwriting — Summer Term

Week 5 — Day 2

Here are some words for you to trace and copy. Start at the red dot each time.

pear

① pear   pear

② bear   bear

③  wear   wear

④ tear   tear

⑤ wears   wears

⑥ wearing

⑦ tearing

How did you find these words with 'ear' in them?

Week 5 — Day 3

Trace over these words, then copy them out.

1. chair   *chair*

2. hair   *hair*

3. fair   *fair*

4. pair   *pair*

5. stairs   *stairs*

6. dairy   *dairy*

7. repair   *repair*

Did you trace and copy these words neatly?

   Year 1 Handwriting — Summer Term

Week 5 — Day 4

Have a go at tracing and copying these words.
They all have 'are' in them.

 care

1. care   *care*

2. dare   *dare*

3. rare   *rare*

4. glare   *glare*

5. scare   *scare*

6. aware   *aware*

7. square   *square*

How did you find these words?

Year 1 Handwriting — Summer Term   © CGP — Not to be photocopied

Week 5 — Day 5

 Time to trace and copy the words and sentence below. They are about Goldilocks and the Three Bears.

bears

chair

 house

golden hair

sleep

Goldilocks ate the porridge.

 Have you been a star with this page?

Year 1 Handwriting — Summer Term

Week 6 — Day 1

Practise these words.
Trace each word before
you copy it out.

1. no   *no*

2. today   *today*

3. they   *they*

4. this   *this*

5. go   *go*

6. so   *so*

7. went   *went*

How did you get on with these words?

Week 6 — Day 2

Trace and then copy each of these words.
They all have 'sk' in them.

(1) ask

(2) sky

(3) mask

(4) skirt

(5) tusk

(6) desk

(7) basket

Did you write these words out neatly?

Year 1 Handwriting — Summer Term

Week 6 — Day 3

Here are some words for you to trace and copy.
Start at the red dot each time.

near

1. near near

2. year year

3. clear clear

4. hear hear

5. gear gear

6. spear spear

7. beard beard

How well do you think you did on this page?

Week 6 — Day 4

Practise writing these words.
Don't forget to start at the red dots.

1. deer *deer*

2. cheer *cheer*

3. peer *peer*

4. steer *steer*

5. career *career*

6. sneer *sneer*

7. *meerkat*

How did you find these words?

Year 1 Handwriting — Summer Term

Week 6 — Day 5

Label these parts of the body.
Trace and then copy each word,
starting at the red dot.

ear

skull

ear

skeleton

hand

skin

foot

leg

How did you get on with writing these labels?

Week 7 — Day 1

Trace and copy each of these words.
The red dots show you where to start.

(1)  **all** all

(2)  **my** my

(3) **there** there

(4) **here** here

(5) **by** by

(6) **some** some

(7) **come** come

How neatly did you write these words?

Week 7 — Day 2

Trace and then copy these words.
Start at the red dot each time.

1. turn   turn

2. nurse   nurse

3. fur   fur

4. church   church

5. hurt   hurt

6. burn   burn

7. burger   burger

Did you write these words neatly?

Week 7 — Day 3

Trace and then copy each of these words.
Don't forget to start at the red dots.

(1) her   her

(2)  flower   flower

(3) kerb   kerb

(4) herd   herd

(5) term   term

(6) person   person

(7) river   river

How did you get on?

   Year 1 Handwriting — Summer Term

Week 7 — Day 4

All of these words end in 'er'.
Trace them and then copy them out.

later

1. later later

2.  letter letter

3. buzzer buzzer

4. paper paper

5. tiger tiger

6. hunter hunter

7. winter winter

How well did you do?

Week 7 — Day 5

Here is a page from a diary.
Trace the words, then copy them out.

Thursday 25th June

It is very hot here today.

I saw a turtle in the water

when I was surfing.

How does your page look?

Year 1 Handwriting — Summer Term

Week 8 — Day 1

First, write over each word.
Then, copy them out.

1. love   love

2. one   one

3. once   once

4. ask   ask

5.  push   push

6. pull   pull

7. full   full

Did you find these words easy or hard?

Week 8 — Day 2

Try tracing and copying these words.
Start each word at the red dot.

 catch

1. catch   catch

2. hatch   hatch

3. patch   patch

4. match   match

5. stitch   stitch

6. witch   witch

7. fetch   fetch

How did you get on with these 'tch' words?

Year 1 Handwriting — Summer Term

Week 8 — Day 3

Practise tracing and copying all of these words.

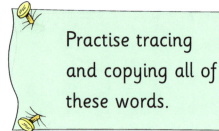

bank

1. bank   bank

2. drink   drink

3. chunk   chunk

4. pink   pink

5. stink   stink

6. think   think

7. thank   thank

Week 8 — Day 4

First trace the words, then copy them out.
These words all have 've' at the end.

1.  give   give

2. have   have

3. brave   brave

4. cave   cave

5. five   five

6. twelve   twelve

7. shave   shave

How did you find this page?

Year 1 Handwriting — Summer Term

Week 8 — Day 5

Trace over this story about fishing.
Then, copy it out underneath.

I love to sit on the bank and

catch fish. Once, I dropped

my rod. Before I could

dive in to fetch it, it sank.

Did you copy the story neatly?

Week 9 — Day 1

Start at the red dots and trace these words. Then, copy them.

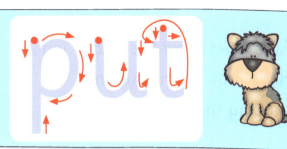

1. put   put

2. school   school

3. made   made

4. house   house

5. our   our

6. into   into

7. today   today

How did you get on with these words?

Year 1 Handwriting — Summer Term

Week 9 — Day 2

All of these words contain 'igh'.
Have a go at tracing and
copying them below.

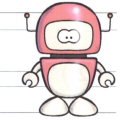

1. might   might

2. light   light

3. high   high

4. right   right

5. tight   tight

6. bright   bright

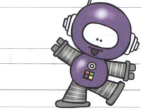

7. sigh   sigh

How did you find these 'igh' words?

Week 9 — Day 3

Today's words all have 'ie' in them.
Remember to start at the dots.

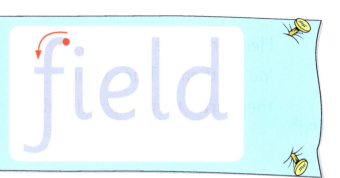

field

1. field   field

2. shield   shield

3. priest   priest

4. chief   chief

5. niece   niece

6. thief   thief

7. piece   piece

Were you able to write all of today's words?

   Year 1 Handwriting — Summer Term

Week 9 — Day 4

Here are some words with 'oa' in them. Trace them, then write them out yourself.

1. coat   coat

 2. goat   goat

3. toast   toast

4. soap   soap

5. road   road

6. loaf   loaf

7. toad   toad

How were these 'oa' words for you?

Week 9 — Day 5

Here is a poster about a school fair. Trace and copy the sentences.

Saturday 8th of June.

Please come to our

school fair! There will be

lots to see and do.

How neat is your poster?

Year 1 Handwriting — Summer Term

Week 10 — Day 1

Here are some words for you to practise. Carefully trace the letters before writing them out yourself.

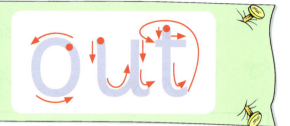

(1) out   out

(2) now   now

(3) have   have

(4) oh   oh

(5) what   what

(6) like   like

(7) when   when

Choose a face to show how today's words went.

Week 10 — Day 2

Trace each word and then copy it out. Start at the red dot each time.

1. Egypt   Egypt

2. myth   myth

3. syrup   syrup

4. symbol   symbol

5. crystal   crystal

6. gymnast

7.  pyramid

How tricky did you find these words?

   Year 1 Handwriting — Summer Term

Week 10 — Day 3

Trace the words and then write them out for yourself.

1. city   city

2. cereal   cereal

3. recipe   recipe

4. spicy   spicy

5. police   police

6. rice   rice

7. dancer   dancer

Did you trace and copy all of these words neatly?

Week 10 — Day 4

These words all end in '-le'.
Trace and then copy them.

1 ankle   ankle

2 apple   apple

3 eagle   eagle

4 turtle   turtle

5 noodle   noodle

6 bubble   bubble

7 little   little

How did you get on with today's words?

   Year 1 Handwriting — Summer Term

Week 10 — Day 5

Trace over the names of the seven shapes below.
Then, copy them out yourself.

(1) circle

(2) square

(3) triangle

(4) rectangle

(5) pyramid

(6) cube

(7) cuboid

How are your shape names looking?

Week 11 — Day 1

Mr and Mrs start with a capital 'M'.
Start with a line going down,
then follow the arrows.

(1) Mrs   Mrs

(2) Mr  Mr

(3) asked   asked

(4) their   their

(5) called   called

(6) looked   looked

(7) could   could

Could you trace and copy these words neatly?

Year 1 Handwriting — Summer Term

Week 11 — Day 2

All these words start with a silent 'k'.
Write the letter 'k' without taking
your pencil off the paper.

(1)  knit *knit*

(2) know *know*

(3) knee *knee*

(4) knock *knock*

(5) knight *knight*

(6) knelt *knelt*

(7) knot *knot*

How did you find tracing and copying this page?

Week 11 — Day 3

Plural means 'more than one'.
Lots of words turn into plurals
when you add an 's' onto the end.
Trace and copy these plural words.

① ships ships

② girls girls

③ cats cats

④ pirates pirates

⑤ books books

⑥ trees trees

⑦ games games

Did you write all of these plural words neatly?

Week 11 — Day 4

Some plural words end in '-es'.
Trace and then copy these '-es' words.

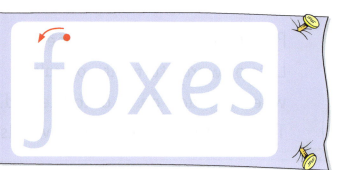

foxes

1) foxes foxes

2) dishes dishes

3) buses buses

4) glasses glasses

5) kisses kisses

6) beaches

7) witches

How did you get on with these '-es' plural words?

Week 11 — Day 5

Trace each line of this rhyme and then copy out the last three lines.

I do not like dogs or cats,

But I do like birds and bats.

I only like animals that fly,

I wish I could join them

in the sky.

Could you neatly trace and copy this rhyme?

Year 1 Handwriting — Summer Term

Week 12 — Day 1

Trace and then copy out the words on this page. Start at the red dot for each word.

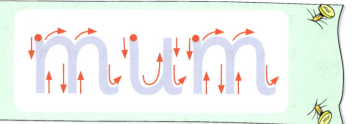

(1) mum   mum

(2) dad   dad

(3) people   people

(4) big   big

(5) little   little

(6) friend   friend

(7) child   child

Did writing out these words go well?

Week 12 — Day 2

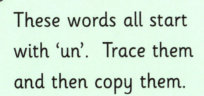

These words all start with 'un'. Trace them and then copy them.

1 unfair ~~unfair~~

2 unzip ~~unzip~~

3 unsafe ~~unsafe~~

4 unkind ~~unkind~~

5 untidy ~~untidy~~

6 unlock ~~unlock~~

7 unfit ~~unfit~~

How do you feel about writing these words?

Year 1 Handwriting — Summer Term

Week 12 — Day 3

Trace and then copy out the words on this page.

① story   story

② fairy   fairy

③ parrot   parrot

④ rabbit   rabbit

⑤ farmer   farmer

⑥ garden   garden

⑦ rocket   rocket

How do the words you have written look?

Week 12 — Day 4

Try tracing and then copying these compound words.

cowboy

1. cowboy

2. pancakes

3. football

4. wheelchair

5. starfish

6. bedroom

7. windmill

How did you do with these compound words?

Year 1 Handwriting — Summer Term

Week 12 — Day 5

These sentences are about who is allowed to go on a slide at a water park. Trace and then copy the sentences.

Mum and Dad are too big

to go on the slide.

Too big

Just right

Too little

My brother is too little.

I am just right.

How do your sentences look?

E1HWSU11